# PERRIAND

Design Monographs

# PERRIAND

DOMINIC LUTYENS

**Charlotte Perriand** | French interior and furniture designer Charlotte Perriand was, for many years, an unsung pioneer of the early twentieth-century modernist movement – she built up her career in a male-dominated world and it has taken decades for her work to be fully appreciated and for her radically innovative ideas to be recognized. For a long time, many world-famous pieces of furniture created by Perriand, or developed in conjunction with fellow designers, were attributed to others.

During her 70-year career, she conceived or popularized many ideas we take for granted today: open-plan residential living, mobile furniture and innovative modular storage units.

Known for espousing machine-age-inspired modernism in the 1920s, she went on to fuse this with an organic aesthetic that reflected her deep-rooted love of nature. Increasingly, she turned to materials such as wood, rushes and bamboo as much as to curvilinear forms, while never entirely jettisoning the crisp clean lines of metal.

Perriand's career – especially early on – mirrored and engaged with current trends in interior design and furniture, notably Art Deco, which thrived in Paris, her birthplace, from the early to mid-1920s. But her designs became more audacious and ground-breaking in the latter half of the decade as she collaborated with such pioneering figures of modernism in France as Le Corbusier and his cousin Pierre Jeanneret. She continued to embrace a modernist style when working with architect and metalworker Jean Prouvé in the late 1930s and again in the postwar years.

Being overshadowed by her male colleagues in the worlds of architecture and design didn't deter her from wholeheartedly pursuing her dream of being a designer – a role which, among her modernist peers, was regarded as heroic in its radical rejection of bourgeois interiors and, as they perceived it, their superfluous ornamentation and clutter.

**Above.** Charlotte Perriand in her Saint-Sulpice studio, Paris, 1928. Le Corbusier's hands hold a plate behind her head like a halo.

# She is definitely one of the most important female designers of the twentieth century – perhaps the most important.
## Justin McGuirk, Former Chief Curator, Design Museum, London

She had an intellectual curiosity that saw her travel to Japan, where she was inspired by its utilitarian and beautifully minimal, traditional interior design and crafts. She plucked elements of Japanese culture and design and fused these with pared-down Western modernism, resulting in a pleasing synthesis of the two.

Her approach was not only forward-looking but international and many of her designs were conceived for different geographical contexts and climates. Increasingly she played with different styles and embraced eclecticism and strong colour which, some might argue, was out of step with doctrinaire modernism, but no less innovative for that. This pluralist approach was particularly evident in several exhibitions of the 1950s, where she showed her furniture alongside art and applied arts by other experimental designers and artists of the time.

She was equally at home designing furniture and homeware fabricated in Japan, intended for export to Western markets, as she was modernist mountain shelters and ski resorts in the French Alps. She also undertook projects in Brazil, the Republic of Guinea, Milan, Geneva and London.

Crucially, her left-wing politics – and belief that good design for all could create a better society – informed her work. Her involvement in the creation of expansive ski resorts in the French Alps was predicated on her view that pleasurable holidays and comfortable accommodation should be widely accessible, not reserved for the rich.

A passion for nature and the great outdoors, deeply ingrained as a result of childhood trips to visit her great-uncle who owned a farm in Burgundy, never

**Above.** La Cascade, Arc 1600, Les Arcs, 1968.

left her: she loved skiing, mountain-climbing and caving. In the 1930s, with Jeanneret and her friend, the artist Fernand Léger, she combed the beaches of Normandy in search of pebbles, textured driftwood and other flotsam and jetsam, dubbing these irregularly shaped objects, *art brut* ("raw art"). She also photographed them, framing and lighting them in such a way that they resembled organic sculptures.

Perriand also trailblazed ecological ideas in master-planning and interior design: the buildings in the high-density skiing resorts she worked on typically hugged the mountain slopes in a way that that minimized their impact on the terrain. They also featured huge windows that blurred the boundaries between inside and out, afforded panoramic views of the landscapes outside and flooded the interiors with natural light.

**Above.** Double Chaise Longue, 1952, shown at the "Charlotte Perriand: The Modern Life" exhibition, Design Museum, London, 2021.

Her sociable personality and taste influenced her work as much as her politics. The radically modern schemes found in her home on Paris's Left Bank, where she was free to try out new ideas in privacy, were recreated at prestigious Paris design fairs, were often well received and then emulated by others. These weren't hypothetical, abstract concepts but real spaces – kitted out, as with her Bar Sous le Toit ("Bar under the Roof"), with a bar and gramophone player – that mirrored her own lifestyle and that of her bohemian friends.

Outgoing, gregarious and generous, she instigated collaborations with like-minded artists, designers and architects, many of whom were close friends. This multidisciplinary approach that fused art, architecture and design was ahead of its time. Perriand was, in turn, held in great affection by some of the eminent figures she worked with; architect Ernő Goldfinger, who co-designed the French Railways office with her in 1963, would sign professional letters to her with love hearts. It wasn't until the 1980s, however, with feminism gaining greater traction, that Perriand became more widely known.

Appropriately, London-based cross-disciplinary collective Assemble, whose work encompasses architecture, design and art, designed the 2021 exhibition "Charlotte Perriand: The Modern Life" at London's Design Museum. Showcasing faithful reconstructions of Perriand-designed interiors, furniture (prototypes and final pieces), sketchbooks and photographs, this show, more so than one held by the same museum in 1996, highlighted the multifaceted nature of her work.

Perriand was born in Paris in 1903, but lived for the first three years of her life on her great-uncle's farm in Moulery (Burgundy), her mother's home village. Her mother directed a couture workshop, while her father sewed for the English tailoring company, Cumberland. During the First World War, Perriand visited her father's family in Savoie, marvelling at its snowy peaks and remarking to relatives that one day she would climb them.

Perriand's extraordinarily independent character in the male-dominated design world can't be put down purely to her spirited personality. Among her contemporaries were a small but significant number of emancipated women designers and artists, notably Eileen Gray and Sonia Delaunay, busy establishing high-profile careers in the early twentieth century, and perhaps this emboldened Perriand to make her mark.

Perriand herself was fortunate to be taken seriously as an artist by female members of her family. Her aunt had attended the school created by the Women's Committee of the Ecole de l'Union Centrale des Arts Décoratifs on the Boulevard Malesherbes, and Perriand obtained a scholarship to study there. Its artistic director, Henri Rapin, was highly supportive of her, while two teachers, Maurice Dufrêne and Paul Follot, introduced her to the nascent Art Deco aesthetic.

Wishing to broaden her art education outside the school, she took drawing classes at the more experimental Académie de la Grande Chaumière and life classes at the studio of French Cubist artist André Lhote. Her enthusiasm for nature was reflected in early drawings. At her great-uncle's farm she made lively sketches of chickens and a detailed study of moths and feathers at the Ecole de l'Union Centrale des Arts Décoratifs.

After the First World War, Paris's major department stores opened their own design studios. Perriand attended one at Galeries Lafayette. One advantage of this system was that its classes were practical and commercial. The students entered competitions and winning entries were often manufactured; Perriand won one competition with a design for a curtain.

While at art school, Perriand produced pieces that were shown at the prestigious 1925 Exposition Internationale des Arts Décoratifs et Industriels Modernes – from which the snappier term Art Deco was originally derived. These comprised a screen depicting the Muses, a wrought-iron grille and a leather binding for Paul Valéry's book *Eupalinos ou l'Architecte*. In 1926 Perriand, with financial help from her parents, exhibited her first ensemble – the term for a fully furnished room set (a new trend in France) – at the Salon des Artistes Décorateurs, an annual event sponsored by the Société des Artistes Décorateurs. She exhibited an armchair, table and bookshelf-cum-writing desk. The latter presaged Perriand's penchant for designing dual-functional, space-saving furniture, although its style was fashionably Art Deco and on-trend rather than experimental. However, she would soon reject the type of luxe, exotic and elitist materials she had used in this *mise-en-scène*, namely amboyna burl and palisander woods, which were commonly associated with Art Deco.

Perriand had considerable freedom for a young woman of the time. At a symposium at the London Institut Français that coincided with the 2021

Design Museum show in London, Perriand's daughter Pernette Perriand-Barsac described how, at the age of eighteen, Charlotte was given complete independence by her mother. Wasting no time in taking full advantage of this opportunity, in 1921 she travelled to Italy with a friend where, Pernette revealed, she met handsome Italian *carabinieri* (as a photograph testifies).

While showing at the Salon des Artistes Décorateurs in 1926, Perriand met Percy Scholefield, who admired her exhibit and snapped it up. He was a friend of Perriand's parents, and twenty years her senior; the two married that year. He supported her career, also buying a silver cabinet with wood painted violet – an indication of her predilection for seductive colour used even in her early, more stark modernist interiors.

The newlyweds moved into a rented former photographer's studio on the bohemian Left Bank, a clear sign that they wished to be part of Paris's thriving community of cutting-edge creatives. Here she discovered the music of Louis Armstrong, learned to dance the Charleston and watched the movies of Jean Cocteau. She was also enraptured by Josephine Baker: she had seen her perform at the Théâtre des Champs-Élysées, and, in 1925, sketched her dancing. One side of the apartment featured an expansive glazed wall overlooking the medieval church of Saint-Sulpice, which sloped upwards near the ceiling, forming a skylight.

The apartment was perfect for socializing. Guests included jeweller and horologist Gérard Sandoz, jewellery designer Jean Fouquet, painter Marianne Clouzot, Surrealist artist Jacqueline Lamba and her new lover, André Breton, co-founder of Surrealism, and photographer Dora Maar (later Pablo Picasso's lover).

In 1927, Perriand recreated one room from the apartment – its bar – at the Salon d'Automne. Naming the exhibit Bar Sous le Toit, it marked a radical departure from the Art Deco opulence of her previous ensembles and was a projection of her own taste, embodying a new, modern lifestyle she embraced from the mid-1920s. She wore her hair in a gamine Eton crop, softened only by flattened, stylized Marcel waves, and sported knee-skimming flapper dresses with bold geometric patterns.

The enticing bar, framed by a boldly angular mansard roof, incorporated a semicircular anodized aluminium cocktail bar hugged by nickel-plated copper

**I think the reason Le Corbusier took me on was because I was familiar with current technology . . . and had ideas about the uses it could be put to.**
Charlotte Perriand

stools. Opposite these stood a chrome-plated table and gramophone cabinet. Steel bands decorated one wall; another bordered the bar. Gone were the overstuffed upholstery and sumptuous, busily layered materials found in Art Deco interiors. Yet mauve and pink leather upholstery on a banquette offset the severity of the reflective metal furniture, conveying an impression of a den devoted to leisure. The attic setting itself was subversive – an anti-bourgeois statement – since attics in Paris traditionally housed *chambres de bonne* ("maid's rooms"). Meanwhile, the challenging metal furniture on display was obviously targeted at the bohemian, urban middle classes, rather than designed to appeal to the more bourgeois and conservative.

That year Perriand began to take a great interest in the work of Swiss-born architect Le Corbusier, who had lived in Paris since 1917 and was heavily influenced by Auguste Perret, a pioneer of the architectural use of reinforced concrete. This began when Fouquet lent her two books by the architect – *Vers Une Architecture* and *L'Art Decoratif d'Aujourd'hui*. As a jewellery designer, Fouquet found himself drawn to such humble components as ball bearings and materials like chrome plating, and soon transitioned from opulent Art Deco styles to a modernist, industrial aesthetic. At the time, Perriand often wore a simple necklace made of ball bearings, perhaps her own creation but possibly a Fouquet design.

At the time, *Vers Une Architecture* was thrillingly compelling – a forward-looking manifesto for modernism, a paean to beauty found in machines and engineering, whose streamlined forms, Le Corbusier believed, could influence and reshape architecture. It featured photographs, drawings, sketches and juxtaposed images of ultra-modern aeroplanes and cars alongside ones of the Parthenon and Notre-Dame. In fact, a photograph of Perriand's apartment with its ultra-modern glass wall overlooking the ancient Saint-Sulpice wouldn't have looked at all out of place in the book.

The books inspired Perriand to apply for a job at Le Corbusier's studio – an unedifying experience. She was turned away by Le Corbusier with the witheringly condescending, oft-quoted words, "We don't embroider cushions here." Not that cushions *per se* were entirely alien to his needs, as things turned out. Ironically, two years later, the supposedly cushion-averse Le Corbusier would give the green light to a new armchair co-created by his cousin Pierre Jeanneret and Perriand – the Fauteuil Grand Confort armchair. At the time, Le Corbusier referred to furniture by the baldly functionalist, matter-of-fact term *équipement*, and held up chairs, tables and storage cabinets found in offices, hospitals and army barracks as exemplars of this new ideal. Yet the Fauteuil Grand Confort featured plump, leather-upholstered cushions, which arguably scarcely conformed to his purist vision of uncompromisingly utilitarian furniture. True, the cushions were firmly encased in the chair's cage-like, cuboid frame, making this rectilinear exoskeleton stand out more, although even this was sprayed pale blue – a softer alternative to bare metal.

Le Corbusier was to change his mind about Perriand on seeing and admiring Bar Sous le Toit at the Salon d'Automne, two months after turning her away from his studio. He was impressed that she had designed bar stools that accorded with this aesthetic and hired the twenty-four-year-old designer to work at his studio on the Rue de Sèvres, putting her in charge of interior design and development of furniture. Perriand was to work for him until 1937 and, during these ten years, Le Corbusier gave her ever greater responsibility.

Furthermore, in 1928, at the Salon des Artistes Décorateurs at the Grand Palais, Perriand exhibited a reproduction of her dining room at home – a radically open-plan space furnished with an extendable, crisply rectilinear dining table and her recently designed swivel armchair, Fauteuil Tournant. The latter, inspired by an early twentieth-century English office chair, featured a cylindrical, Michelin Man-esque, leather-upholstered backrest and cushioned seat in an eye-catching oxblood shade. Her room – in an area also featuring spaces designed by avant-garde furniture designer and architect René Herbst and architect and interior designer Djo-Bourgeois – was clutter-free and audaciously illuminated by a car headlight acquired at the Salon de l'Automobile. There wasn't a hint of formality about the dining table: it hadn't been smothered by a tablecloth and was laid only with simple wine glasses, plates and cutlery.

Incidentally, it presumably didn't escape Le Corbusier's notice that Perriand's swivelling Fauteuil Tournant added a new dimension to the existing repertoire of tubular metal furniture – it was kinetic.

To date, Le Corbusier had furnished his projects with bentwood pieces made by manufacturer Thonet – the most functionalist furniture he could get his hands on at the time, but an unsatisfactory compromise. Despite promising his construction supervisor, Alfred Roth, steel furniture to include in exhibitions, Le Corbusier only got as far as creating drawings illustrating seating that could accommodate various body positions, including work/dining, conversation and relaxing. He believed that henceforth domestic chairs should be lower, taking their cue from club chairs, deckchairs and car seats.

German company Standard-Möbel, Lengyel & Company had produced Marcel Breuer's early tubular steel furniture inspired by bicycle handlebars, yet France lacked a manufacturer of tubular metal furniture. When Le Corbusier saw examples of it by Breuer, Mies van der Rohe and Dutch architect and furniture designer Mart Stam at the "Die Wohnung" ("The Dwelling") exhibition that showcased radically innovative housing in Stuttgart in 1927, he became painfully aware that he had a lot of catching up to do.

Soon after, with Jeanneret, Perriand developed two more chairs – the Siège à Dossier Basculant and Chaise Longue Basculante. Along with the Fauteuil Grand Confort, these are now widely recognized as twentieth-century design classics. With these pieces, Perriand and Jeanneret explored the idea of kinetic furniture further. The Siège à Dossier Basculant, a modern reworking of an officer's chair, had a swinging back.

**Opposite.** Perriand's dining room, later recreated at the Salon des Artistes Décorateurs, Grand Palais, 1928.

**The upright Salon hadn't expected its galleries to bubble with such brazen youth.**
Charlotte Perriand

Resourceful and practical, Perriand sourced the materials for these chairs from hardware shops and department stores and supervised their execution. She sought out ponyskin from furriers, and used it to cover the chaise longue, which also incorporates a bolster to cushion the head. Here was another unexpectedly luxurious touch given Le Corbusier's distaste for bourgeois comfort, although the ponyskin wasn't overtly opulent since it covered the chaise longue with a thin, light layer. The chaise longue – a contemporary take on a traditional rocking chair – took the idea of moveable elements a stage further. Supported by a stable base, its moveable upper frame could be repositioned; its angle could be adjusted according to the sitter's needs.

Perriand was photographed more than once on the chaise longue, reclining at different angles, presumably to demonstrate how it could be repositioned. These images of the recumbent designer, in a knee-length skirt, hair neatly short and gamine, have since become iconic – emblematic of the

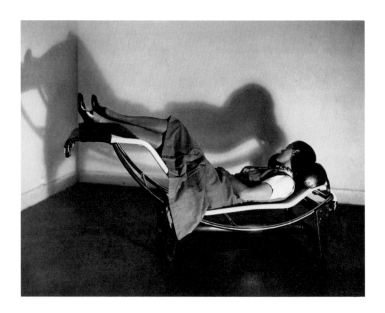

**Above.** Perriand on the Chaise Longue Basculante, 1928.

modern woman in the modernist age. With her face turned enigmatically away from the camera, the images have a Surrealist quality – redolent of Man Ray's photographs – and highlight Perriand's connections with Surrealism. Besides being a friend of André Breton, Perriand took a series of Surrealist-inflected, *art brut* photographs of found, natural objects – driftwood or bones – in the 1930s.

There was, however, an anomaly between the intention behind the milestone-marking chairs produced at Le Corbusier's studio and the outcome. The designs and their machine-age aesthetic were inspired by mass-production and Taylorism (a factory management system developed in the late nineteenth century to increase efficiency by breaking down production into specialized, repetitive tasks), and the hope was that the new chairs, too, could be mass-produced and be widely accessible. Yet the pieces, fabricated at first by Thonet, ended up in the homes of wealthy bourgeois bohemians. The Siège à Dossier Basculant, for example, graced several Le Corbusier villas commissioned by affluent clients, including Villa Savoye in Poissy, near Paris, completed in 1931.

Even so, the metal chairs – unveiled in a compact apartment setting at the Salon d'Automne in December 1929 – publicly proclaimed Le Corbusier's allegiance to the brave new world of machine-age modernism. Perriand had already laid her cards on the table in her article for British magazine *The Studio* – with its headline, "Wood or Metal?" and its evangelical refrain, "METAL plays the same part in furniture as cement has done in architecture" – in which she unapologetically stated her preference for metal. The feature was in fact an outspoken riposte to a previously published piece in *The Studio* lambasting the use of metal in furniture.

Le Corbusier's studio planned to show its new metal furniture collection at the exhibition of the Salon des Artistes Décorateurs, but when it was presented to the jury in May 1929, it was rejected. Perriand promptly resigned from the Salon and joined the Union des Artistes Modernes. Instead, the collection had its first public airing in the setting of a radically open-plan apartment at the Salon d'Automne, funded by Thonet. This gave context to the furniture, which was shown in a compact space that measured 9 metres (29$^1$/$_2$ feet) by 10 metres (33 feet) and dominated by a living room on two floors. On the lower level were a kitchen, bathroom and two sleeping areas, the latter simply

# Without well-planned storage, it is impossible to find space in one's home.
Charlotte Perriand

separated from the living space by metal storage cabinets. The floor was made of glass slabs laid in sand. Not only did the space's hard-edged, almost clinical forms and unyielding surfaces challenge many visitors' preconceptions of how a domestic interior should look, but walls normally guaranteeing privacy between household members were shockingly absent: the bathing area and two sleeping areas formed one continuous space. This emphasis on bathing accorded with the modernist concern for hygiene (extolled in Perriand's article for *The Studio*). Yet many visitors to the fair might have aspired to own its evidently luxurious cylindrical shower unit.

The apartment also promoted flexibility and mobility in the form of sliding doors, while the bed rested on ball bearings, so it could be moved. However, the chairs came to be prefaced with the letters "LC", denoting that they were part of a collection attributed to Le Corbusier's studio. This obscured the important role Perriand had played in their creation, and given the chairs' lastingly iconic status, this partly explains the scant acclaim Perriand has garnered for many years. It is only in the past two decades that her influence has been more widely acknowledged – and fêted. In 2019–20, Fondation Louis Vuitton in Paris celebrated her seventy-year career with a huge exhibition distributed over four floors.

With a sudden change in the political and economic climate triggered by the Wall Street crash of 1929 and the advent, in the 1930s, of Nazism in Germany, Fascism in Italy, Stalinism in the USSR and Franco's dictatorship in Spain, the bombastic triumphalism of machine-age modernism started to feel inappropriate.

More specifically, in the case of Le Corbusier's studio, the realization that its metal furniture had a limited audience, due partly to a reluctance by French manufacturers to mass-produce it, may have left the team questioning its relevance. Not that the studio didn't try to court manufacturers: Perriand approached French car-maker Peugeot to see if it might fabricate the furniture, to no avail. In 1933, as Hitler rose to power in Germany, Thonet granted licences for its manufacture to foreign companies, but sales declined dramatically. By 1937, production of the collection ceased and only resumed after the Second World War; initially it was solely attributed to Le Corbusier. In 1959, his Zurich gallerist Heidi Weber began producing the chairs, before Italian company Cassina acquired the licence to manufacture them in 1965 under the direction of Charlotte Perriand and Fondation Le Corbusier.

As the 1930s progressed, Perriand became increasingly independent as a designer, although she would collaborate with Le Corbusier in the future. In 1932, by now having split from Scholefield, she opened her own studio in Montparnasse, Paris. Meanwhile, her late 1920s espousal of a strict, homogeneously industrial aesthetic was waning and giving way to an appreciation of a variety of materials – including wooden furniture hand-crafted by carpenters – and the cultivation of a more eclectic aesthetic.

Particularly inventive examples of this new direction were Perriand's free-form wood tables, desks and sideboards, created from 1937 to 1939.

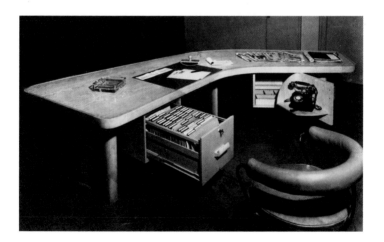

**Above.** The Bureau Boomerang desk, designed by Perriand for Jean-Richard Bloch, 1938.

A germ of this idea can be seen in her wooden, sculptural En Forme Libre table, launched, surprisingly, in 1928. Rustic overtones can be seen in the generously curved edges of its top and its chunky legs. While apparently turning her back on the machine-age aesthetic, especially when designing her asymmetric, free-form pieces, Perriand didn't eschew functionality. She was nothing if not practical, and even her free-form furniture was still functional, albeit in a more subtle, less conspicuous way.

Perriand also furnished some of her projects with overtly rustic rush-seat or rattan chairs; the latter graced her design, Maison du Jeune Homme ("House for a Young Man"), shown at the Brussels International Exhibition of 1935. The room, incidentally, had a playful feel typical of much of her work. Aside from a study area with a desk, it boasted gymnastic equipment, including pull-up rings and a trapeze bar – a space any industrious yet athletic young man could wish for and one that reflected Perriand's love of sport.

In 1938, she was commissioned to refurbish the Paris office of Jean-Richard Bloch, editor-in-chief of Communist newspaper Ce Soir. Its main feature and focal point was its monumental, asymmetric desk, shaped like a boomerang, which gives it its name. The expansive desk with a wide top for spreading out newspapers, notepads and so on, was designed for editorial meetings. Bloch's colleagues could sit opposite him, around the desk's semicircular outer edge, in a non-hierarchical way. The table rested on three legs spaced widely apart, providing plenty of leg room. And Bloch's chair? Perriand's modestly sized, enduringly appealing Fauteuil Tournant of 1927, which allowed Bloch to turn and face any of his colleagues easily.

Perriand also designed versatile wooden dining tables with sides of varying lengths, giving sitters the choice to sit together intimately, if seated on the shorter sides, or further apart, on the longer sides. Again these had three legs, allowing sitters to move their legs freely. The tables were also ergonomic as they had smooth, rounded edges that were soft to the touch.

Such designs, which reflected Perriand's deep-rooted love of nature, were inseparable from her commitment to environmentalism. She was an extraordinarily pioneering advocate of this cause, which was a key issue addressed by her 1936 photomontage, La Grande Misère de Paris ("Poverty-stricken Paris"), co-created with younger architects Jean Bossu, Émile Enci,

Jacques Woog and Georges Pollak. This confrontational frieze – an unmissable, hard-hitting critique of squalid, unsafe living conditions in Paris that combined images and consciousness-raising text – was shown that year at the Salon des Arts Ménagers at the Grand Palais.

A crucial, concurrent influence on Perriand's development as a designer was her politicization, which led to her think, perhaps more deeply than before, about the purpose of design. It was no longer enough, nor ethically acceptable, for designers to content themselves with creating revolutionary furniture, intended to *épater les bourgeois* at prestigious public fairs. Such thinking was elitist and shallow. Instead, Perriand now felt that the raison d'être of architecture and design was to benefit society as a whole. Architects and designers henceforth had a responsibility to better the world and to democratize design, making it accessible to as many people as possible, not just to a wealthy elite.

Aside from a realization that only a privileged few had access to the elegant furniture issued by Le Corbusier's studio, other factors caused Perriand to become *engagée* (the French term for politically engaged). In 1931, she joined the Association des Écrivains et Artistes Révolutionnaires (AEAR), which was affiliated to the French Communist Party. This association, active between 1932 and 1939, was founded by Communist and Communist-sympathizing writers and artists.

From 1935, Perriand participated in activities organized by the Maison de la Culture, an offshoot of the association. She was also a member of the Congrès Internationaux d'Architecture Moderne (CIAM). Co-founded in 1928 by 28 European architects, including Le Corbusier, Gerrit Rietveld and Pierre Chareau, and disbanded in 1959, CIAM held events and conferences in Europe whose delegates included prominent architects. Their goal was to promote the principles of the modern movement in a variety of fields, from architecture to industrial design.

Feeding into her work and expanding her experience and cultural horizons were the many trips Perriand took abroad from the 1930s onwards, initially through her association with CIAM. She attended two CIAM conferences in Moscow in 1931 and 1934 and one in Athens in 1933.

Around this time, Perriand was also inspired by Catalan architect Josep Lluís Sert, a former assistant of Le Corbusier who co-founded the Group of

Catalan Artists and Technicians for the Progress of Contemporary
Architecture (GATCPAC), the Spanish branch of CIAM. Sert built social
housing and holiday homes, including at Garraf, a seaside village near Sitges
in Catalonia. The latter were simple, flat-roofed structures, the bases of which
were clad with large stones creating a rustic, organic effect that allowed the
houses to blend with the surrounding rugged landscape. So, too, did outdoor
terraces that capitalized on the coastal views. The houses' interiors were

> # Everything changes so quickly and what is state-of-the-art one moment won't be the next. Adaptation has to be ongoing ... these are transient times.
> Charlotte Perriand

uncluttered and sparsely and simply furnished with rustic chairs and tables and modernist armchairs.

Perriand designed a series of structures geared for leisure in the 1930s, a move that chimed with a growing belief in the right of the working classes to paid holidays. In 1936, in France, the newly elected Front Populaire introduced a law mandating twelve weeks' paid annual leave for workers. Before 1936, only professionals, *rentiers* (individuals who earned income from investments) and traders took holidays in France. Most workers did not get paid if they did not work, only resting on Sundays. By the end of that year, more than 600,000 wage earners and their families holidayed away from home; the following year that number had tripled.

Ideologically, Perriand clashed with Le Corbusier over the introduction of paid vacations for workers. He feared that any pause in mechanized manufacturing would release people from factories onto the streets and result in anarchy. But Perriand saw the new law in a positive light. She associated leisure hours with an opportunity for city-dwellers to escape insanitary urban housing and commune with nature and so live healthier lives.

Of course, this socially progressive legislation necessitated housing for holiday-makers – and on a mass scale. Her solution, along with Sert's, was prefabricated dwellings, and prefabricated architecture and design soon

**Opposite.** Perriand with Le Corbusier, 1928.

became a major preoccupation of Perriand, particularly in her collaborations with French architect, designer and metalworker Jean Prouvé. In 1939, just before the outbreak of war, she designed prefabricated military barracks and furniture for temporary housing for his studio, Ateliers Jean Prouvé. She also took charge of the creation of temporary structures for workers who were constructing an aluminium-manufacturing factory in Issoire, central France, designed by Auguste Perret. Short of time to undertake the project, Perriand opted to use prefabricated units.

Perriand's earliest ideas for holiday homes didn't exactly meet a need for mass housing – a concern she addressed extensively with her ski resort projects in the French Alps from the 1960s to the 1980s – but they at least celebrated the desire to unwind, relax and have fun. One of these projects, La Maison au Bord de l'Eau, was a design she submitted in 1934 for a competition to design an inexpensive weekend house, organized by *L'Architecture d'Aujourd'hui*, a magazine co-founded by Le Corbusier in 1930. Arguably, her weekend retreat recalls the hedonistic Bar Sous le Toit in that

**Above.** La Maison au Bord de l'Eau, designed in 1934, built by Louis Vuitton in 2013.

this waterside bolthole was also dedicated to leisure, thanks to its outdoor terrace intended for sunbathing, alfresco meals, dancing and other activities. In this respect, there's a continuity between the two projects. Yet in other ways they clearly differ: La Maison au Bord de l'Eau made a feature of wood, not metal. And, unlike the unmistakably urban Bar Sous le Toit, La Maison au Bord de l'Eau was destined for rural settings.

The latter – which was reminiscent of oyster farmers' huts on the Île aux Oiseaux in the Bassin d'Arcachon on the west coast of France, where Perriand spent the summer of 1934 with Jeanneret and Le Corbusier – also illustrates Perriand's prescient interest in environmentalism. It comprised an outdoor terrace sandwiched between two symmetrical structures, all supported by stilts, and was designed to be easy to assemble and disassemble. The building, conceived as suitable for almost any terrain, came in kit form. It comprised prefabricated panels for floors, walls, ceilings and partitions, and didn't require permanent foundations. As such, it avoided making a lasting, negative impact on the environment.

The project also echoed Perriand's personal exploration of flexible, modular structures, since it could be enlarged if the family using it grew, or its needs changed over the years. What's more, the height of the stilts could be adjusted to provide extra room under the structure to house a cellar, garage or workshop.

From 1934 to 1938, Perriand also designed mountain lodges as well as her Bivouac and Tonneau mountain refuges – other examples of her personal passions, in this case for skiing and mountain-climbing, overlapping with her work. Bivouac, co-created with engineer André Tournon, was exhibited on the banks of the Seine in Paris, during the 1937 Exposition Internationale des Arts et Techniques dans la Vie Moderne (International Exhibition of Art and Technology in Modern Life). The design was modified soon after by Jeanneret. It was shown in the Pavilion des Temps Nouveaux, designed by Le Corbusier and Jeanneret, and project-managed by Perriand.

Bivouac was a dress rehearsal for the more practical and homely, two-storey Tonneau refuge of 1938, which took its name from the French for "barrel" (*tonneau*) – hence its faceted façade, which was designed to resist strong winds. It was originally inspired by a merry-go-round photographed in

Croatia in 1937. On the face of it, with its glistening exterior made of insulating aluminium, the futuristic, idiosyncratic Tonneau recalled Perriand's veneration of metal in the 1920s. Yet, in stark contrast to its exterior, the inside was lined with warm-looking wood. While compact, its 3.8-metre (12$^1$/$_5$-foot) diameter interior, which could sleep eight people, wasn't cramped.

The entire prefabricated structure, which also resembled a cross between a spaceship and a giant musical box, was designed to be easily portable. It was available as sections that could be carried in backpacks all the way up to a snowy summit. To that end, no single component was to weigh more than 40 kilogrammes (88 pounds) or exceed 1.05 metres (3$^1$/$_2$ feet) by 2.1 metres (6$^3$/$_4$ feet), as Bivouac's elements had done. Those who made it to a suitable mountain spot (although Tonneau was designed to be erected on other types of terrains, too) could refer to an instruction manual featuring photos of different construction stages. The advent of the Second World War, however, prevented the structure from being built. (In 2012, Cassina created a life-sized reconstruction of the shelter, based on Perriand's drawings and notes.)

While working on the Bivouac shelter, Perriand and Jeanneret stayed in a hotel where she came up with many ideas for mountain chalet interiors, such as dissolving the boundaries between inside and out thanks to large windows and terraces, embracing rustic forms and craft techniques and including her free-form tables.

A multitude of issues that concerned Perriand coalesced in *La Misère de Paris*, which highlights another recurrent aspect of her work: her interest in supersized, two-dimensional, often photographic images used as one of many elements in an interior (she included dramatic, large-scale photographic images in some of the interiors she created for Air France's tourist offices, for example). The same went for her integration of paintings and wall-mounted art by Fernand Léger, Georges Braque, Pablo Picasso, Alexander Calder, Pierre Soulages and Hans Hartung into some of her interior design projects over the years.

The enormous, immersive photomontage, *La Misère de Paris*, almost extended from floor to ceiling and measured over 15 metres (50 feet) long. Its dynamic contrasts of scale, evocative of cinematic jump cuts, and bold typography reflected her familiarity with and understanding of the visual language and collage techniques deployed by the Russian Constructivists,

**Perriand was a natural collaborator . . . For Perriand collaboration is a natural, productive and social way of working.**
Justin McGuirk, Former Chief Curator, Design Museum, London

such as Alexander Rodchenko and El Lissitzky, whose arresting graphic style she had encountered and absorbed in the USSR. The frieze collaged photographs taken by herself with others she'd collected – and included bursts of bright colour alongside black and white photographs that, by contrast, looked appropriately sooty, almost grimy. While decrying poverty, insalubrious housing, pollution, urban sprawl, overcrowding, the wanton destruction of nature and alienation (the theory expounded upon by Karl Marx that human life was rendered worthless by a modern capitalist system), the frieze wasn't didactic. Instead, it was bitingly ironic.

True, it unequivocally drew attention to such issues as high rates of child mortality in the city, while a large map of Paris pinpointed the capital as the source of social ills. It flagged up that humanity was making technical and industrial advances but that the very workers facilitating them were not benefiting from such so-called progress. Workers were forced to live in squalid conditions, often with no running water, while housewives were doing a double day of work – both toiling in factories and slaves to housework at home (an early indication of Perriand's feminist sympathies). And by highlighting how industry was despoiling nature, she voiced proto-eco sentiments. Even so, the photomontage's surreal play on scale and non-linear fragments of text defied an easy reading.

Despite her strong Communist convictions, in 1939, like many other left-wing designers, Perriand broke from the Communist Party in disgust at the German–Soviet Nonaggression Pact (the Molotov-Ribbentrop Pact), signed in August that year just before Germany and the USSR invaded Poland. The pact saw the two countries agree not to attack each other and they secretly divided up Eastern Europe between them.

Soon after the outbreak of the Second World War, Perriand received an unexpected invitation that would take her far from Europe. In early 1940, she opened a letter from the Japanese embassy in Paris asking her to serve as a consultant in industrial design to the Department of Trade Promotion under the auspices of the Ministry of Commerce and Industry in Japan. The ministry hoped that a new foreign advisor could boost Japan's export of furniture and homeware by coming up with contemporary designs that would prove hugely popular with consumers in North America and Europe.

In the 1930s, foreign demand for traditional Japanese wares including silk, which had once been highly coveted, went into sharp decline because of the Depression of the 1930s and the rising popularity of modern, synthetic materials. Adding to Japan's economic woes were anti-Japanese feelings in the West, with boycotts of exports from Japan imposed by French and British ports in 1938 as a result of Japanese expansionism in China. It therefore became essential, in a bid to improve the nation's faltering economy, for Japan to generate its own covetable exportable goods using indigenous materials and craft techniques.

Perriand had a contact in Japan who recommended her for the role – modernist architect Junzo Sakakura, a former colleague and skiing companion who'd worked with her at Le Corbusier's studio. Industrial designer Sōri Yanagi, employed at the time by an organization promoting Japanese exports, initially wanted to invite Le Corbusier to fill the role but Sakakura suggested Perriand instead. Sōri – who would design his classic, sensually curvaceous Butterfly stool some years later, in 1954 – was the son of Sōetsu Yanagi, a co-founder of Japan's Mingei movement. Founded in the 1920s, this aimed to preserve and promote fast-disappearing crafts traditionally practised in the country's small towns and villages. Just as Perriand had admired French peasant crafts, she felt an affinity with the Mingei movement (sometimes translated into English as "folk crafts").

Escaping Paris the day after the German army captured the city in June 1940, she boarded the Japanese cargo ship *Hakusan Maru*, immersing herself during the voyage in Okakura Kakuzō's *The Book of Tea* of 1906, which profoundly influenced her. It describes the Japanese tea ceremony in detail, explaining how its rituals blend with traditional Japanese life, while also contesting stereotypical Western views of the East. Initially based in Tokyo, she wasted no time in closely studying Japanese crafts and materials. With Sōri as her travelling companion, she visited bamboo-working and straw-weaving workshops. She also lectured at art schools.

**Above.** A selection of Perriand's work at the "Selection, Tradition, Creation" exhibition, Japan, 1941.

Stepping into an economically sober, constrained climate, the resourceful Perriand investigated the potential of using inexpensive materials to develop new products. During 1940 and 1941, she regularly attended lectures that explored the possibilities of adapting local craftwork to a contemporary urban lifestyle using straw, rush, bamboo and tree bark, with the practical aid of craftspeople. Her research culminated in her curating several exhibitions in the country.

Overall, while in Japan Perriand benefited from her wide-ranging exposure to Japan's traditional arts and crafts and culture, while she encouraged Japanese modernists and the Japanese public to appreciate their own peasant crafts. Arguably, she inspired Japanese designers, such as Isamu Noguchi, whose globally popular 1950s Akari lights – still in demand today – fused ancient lantern-making techniques with an understated modernist aesthetic.

In 1941, she organized exhibitions that presented the fruits of her research in the high-end Takashimaya department stores in Tokyo and Osaka. (Japan's department stores were as influential in showcasing desirable design as those in Paris where a young Perriand had acquired some of her skills.) One of her exhibitions, called "Selection, Tradition, Creation", displayed work inspired by Mingei arts and crafts, which she deemed suitable for export. These pared-back products chimed with Perriand's modernist sensibility. She also showed some of her own designs, such as a 1940 bamboo and wood iteration of the iconic 1920s Chaise Longue Basculante. Inspired by some elegant Japanese bamboo sugar tongs she happened to see and admire, this similarly adjustable adaptation using bamboo was clever and apt: resting on a rigid oak and beech base, the seat and backrest were, by contrast, made of strips of bamboo that were gently pliable and so moulded to the body. She also exhibited her designs for a bed and sofa, also fashioned from bamboo.

Perriand's curatorial approach with her shows in Japan was counter-intuitive – in Japan at the time, department stores emulated their Western counterparts, while well-heeled, fashionable consumers aspired to acquire Western fashion and homeware.

Despite her affinity with traditional Japanese crafts, Perriand openly criticized a lot of Japanese design created for export at the time. She observed that much of it aped superannuated, historicist Western styles in

**Above.** Hinoki cypress wood table and wool rug, shown at the "Proposal for a Synthesis of the Arts" exhibition, Tokyo, 1955.

the misguided view that these would appeal to the European market. She believed instead that the Japanese should draw from their own traditions and reinvent them in order to come up with fresh ideas.

Despite the immense deference shown in Japan towards Perriand, as demonstrated by one show she organized there, entitled "An Exhibition of Madame Perriand's Works: A Suggestion of Interior Equipment for the House of the Year 2601 – Utilization of the Materials and Techniques Available under Wartime Circumstances", she also ruffled a few feathers.

Japan's more avant-garde industrial designers admonished her for her curatorial selections. In their view she was guilty of a misty-eyed, romanticized vision of the Mingei tradition. By focusing so much on bamboo, she had failed to showcase a whole raft of other cutting-edge materials that were being developed in Japan at the time. Not that it was to be her last sojourn in Japan: in 1955, she staged the show "Proposal for a Synthesis of the Arts, Paris 1955, Le Corbusier, Fernand Léger, Charlotte Perriand", held at the Takashimaya department store in Tokyo. A truly collaborative endeavour, it united architecture, furniture, art, tableware, tapestries, ceramics and jewellery. This eclectic *mise-en-scène* incorporated work by Le Corbusier and Léger as well as her own pieces, among them free-form tables and aluminium storage cabinets fabricated by Ateliers Jean Prouvé.

I would be very happy if you could contribute to the practical structural aspects of the settings which are within your domain, that is to say the knack of a practical woman, talented and kind at the same time.
Le Corbusier

**Above.** The exterior of the French government tourist office, London, 1962.

**Above.** Perriand overlooking mountains, 1930.

Her fascination with Japan proved enduring. In 1993, she designed a tea house for the Cultural Festival of Japan in Paris. Referencing her cherished *The Book of Tea*, she encircled her pavilion with tall bamboo plants, thereby cutting it off from the city, allowing visitors to meditate in this peaceful space, as Perriand intended. Its translucent green roof reinforced the illusion for visitors of being immersed in nature.

In 1942, Perriand travelled to French Indochina, where she lectured on industrial design in Hanoi. On her return to Japan she was put under surveillance and that year her appointment was terminated. She then moved again to Indochina. While there, she married second husband Jacques Martin and gave birth to their daughter, Pernette. In 1946, Perriand returned to Paris.

Perriand was certainly not short of work after the Second World War, nor indeed during the post-war years. She was busy until her death in 1999. Aged ninety-three, she attended the opening night of her show at London's Design Museum in 1996. The same year, she received an honorary doctorate from the Royal College of Art in London. In 1998, she published her autobiography, *Une Vie de Création*.

Long before that, soon after returning to France following the war, Perriand reconnected with Le Corbusier and Jeanneret. Fifty major cities had been badly bombed and the country was undergoing reconstruction on a vast scale. A key reconstruction project was Le Corbusier's building, L'Unité d'Habitation, in Marseille. Perriand wrote to him, offering to contribute to it. His reply was as patronizing as when he turned her down for a job in 1927: "I do not think it would be interesting, now that you're a mother ... to oblige you to be present in the atelier." But it seemed that he needed – and rated her

I love mountains because they are vital to my wellbeing. They have always been the barometer of my physical and moral equilibrium.
Charlotte Perriand

– more than he was prepared to admit: "On the other hand, I would be very happy if you could contribute to the practical structural aspects of the settings which are within your domain, that is to say the knack of a practical woman, talented and kind at the same time." Perriand came up trumps, designing compact modular kitchens integrated into open-plan living areas. This socially progressive concept, ensuring that women weren't sequestered in the kitchen, was another indication of her feminist values.

In 1950, she was assigned an important role at Ateliers Jean Prouvé; she was made artistic director of the furniture department, put in charge of making aesthetic and practical improvements to existing designs and expected to contribute new ideas.

In 1951, she became a member of a group called Espace, founded by sculptor André Bloc, which aimed to fuse the ideals of Constructivism (co-founded by Rodchenko and Vladimir Tatlin) and Neo-plasticism – a term adopted by artist Piet Mondrian – with architecture. With other members of the group, who included Sonia Delaunay and Victor Vasarely, she designed furniture for two student halls of residence at the Cité Internationale Universitaire de Paris – Maison de la Tunisie and Maison du Mexique. Her pieces, which included geometric bookcases fronted by vibrantly coloured rectangular sliding panels, fabricated by Ateliers Jean Prouvé, appropriately nodded to Mondrian's abstract canvases.

From 1957, Perriand embarked on several interior design projects for the tourist offices of Air France, for which her husband worked. Prior to this, Air France hired her to create the interiors of a housing block for the staff of its office in Brazzaville, in the Republic of the Congo. In these she often installed scaled-up, two-dimensional imagery (redolent in terms of size of her photomontage, *La Grande Misère de Paris*), adding greater visual impact to spaces kitted out with ultra-modern furniture.

Aside from the image of Perriand reclining on the 1920s chaise longue, another striking photograph from around 1930 shows her topless, arms exultantly raised towards the sky, a vista of mountains stretching into the distance. The image is a reminder of her passion for skiing and mountain-climbing. In 1961, she designed her own, two-storey chalet at Méribel Les Allues which, in characteristic Perriand style, boasted spacious, open-plan interiors. Its windows had double-glazed, sliding panes that maximized views of the landscape and let in plenty of daylight and fresh air.

Also in 1961, developer Roger Godino and ski instructor Robert Blanc found a site in the French Alps, and had the idea of creating a ski resort they called Les Arcs. Godino visited Perriand at her Méribel chalet and asked her to lead the group of architects hired to work on this mammoth project. She oversaw the creation of three of its modernist villages – Arc 1600, Arc 1800 and Arc 2000 (the figures refer to the altitudes of each village) – which allowed the resort to expand over time.

This, her largest, most ambitious and final project, was constructed from the 1960s to the 1980s, and during this time Perriand was in her element. In her complexes of chalets incorporating other amenities, key themes in her work coalesced – her love of nature, her concern for environmentalism, her democratic belief that design should be available to all and feminism (or at least feminist sentiments). Interestingly, in 1950 French *Elle* magazine envisaged a ministerial government made up wholly of women (in France, women finally gained the right to vote in 1944, and had the first opportunity to do so in the elections of 1945). Perriand, who agreed to take part, was designated to be Minister of Reconstruction. Asked what her goals would be in that position, she stressed the urgency of completing housing, schools and hospitals.

In contrast to many ski resorts, Les Arcs' two-to-five-bedroom apartments, which include affordable rental units, don't encroach on the landscape. Admittedly, they were built on a greenfield site. But, as with the resort's most iconic complex, La Cascade, which accommodates over 1,000 residents, its angled blocks sensitively follow the topography of the terrain, leaning into rather than looming over the slopes. Each unit has a large terrace that catches the sun. The apartments' open-plan living rooms, simply furnished with blond pine tables and built-in storage units, incorporate kitchens with a worktop facing the living space, which ensured that women (at the time the chalets were first inhabited, when gender roles were more fixed) weren't confined to a separate cooking area.

Another ecological, visionary aspect of Les Arcs is that it was conceived as a car-free area; cars are banished to the outskirts of the resort. For

# There is no formula for design. I learned, and above all realized that nothing should be excluded. Charlotte Perriand

Perriand, a one-time champion of machine-worshipping modernism, this was something of a turnaround.

Perriand is a designer who is hard to categorize. She initially appeared to follow design trends – in particular Art Deco – but then engaged with and helped to pioneer one of the more iconoclastic movements of the twentieth century – modernism. Over time, she became an increasingly individual designer who, thanks to her open, enquiring mind and exploration of new materials and forms, developed her own design language. She was extraordinarily ahead of her time, finding ways in which architecture and design could make a practical, positive difference to the world – and implementing them. Above all, she ensured design was never divorced from reality, that it met both human and social needs.

**Opposite.** Arc 1800, Les Arcs, 1974.
**Overleaf.** Perriand at the "Synthesis of the Arts" exhibition, Tokyo, 1955.

[01, 02, 03, 04] La Maison au Bord de l'Eau, designed in 1934, built by Louis Vuitton in 2013.

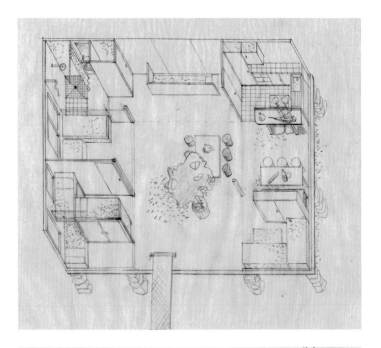

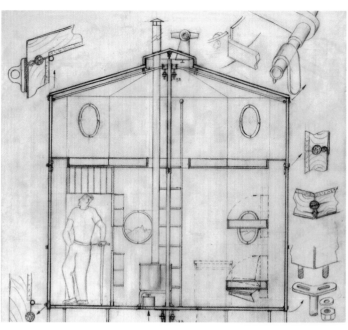

[05, 06] Perriand's drawings of the layout and interiors of La Maison au Bord de l'Eau, 1934.
[07, 08] Le Refuge Tonneau, designed in collaboration with Pierre Jeanneret, 1938.
[09] Miravidi, Arc 1800, Les Arcs, 1974.

[10] South Slopes, Arc 1600, Les Arcs, 1968. [11] La Cachette, Arc 1600, Les Arcs, 1968.
[12] Belles Challes, Arc 1800, Les Arcs, 1974.

[14]

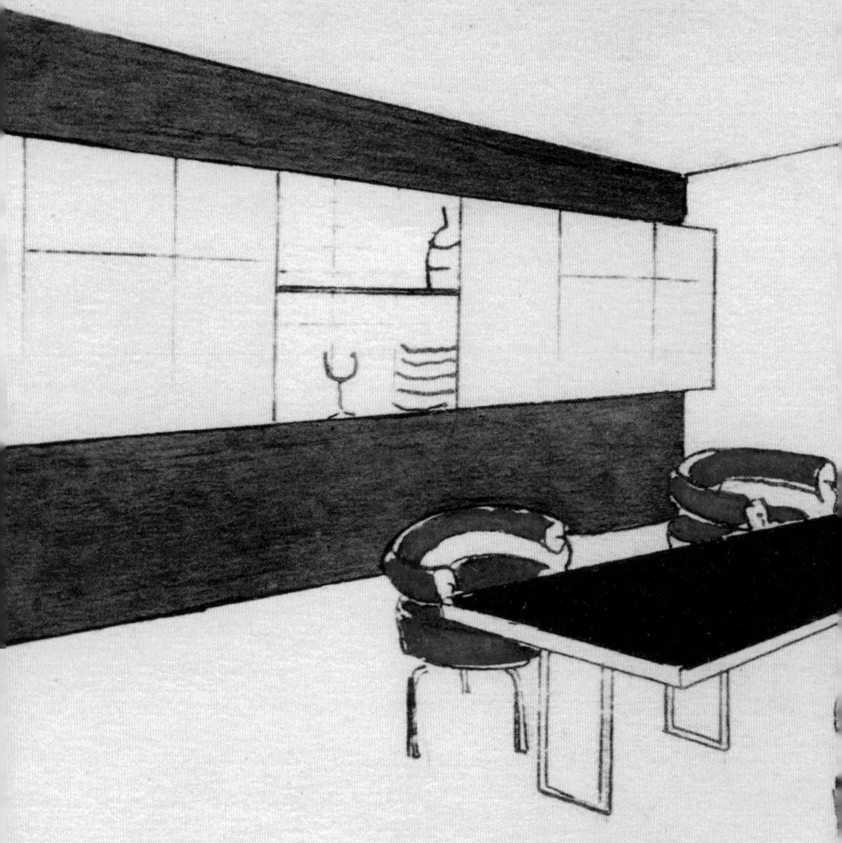

**[13]** Bar Sous le Toit, Salon d'Automne, Paris, 1927. **[14]** Perriand's drawing of her apartment in Saint-Sulpice, Paris, 1927. **[15]** Equipment Intérieur d'une Habitation, designed with Le Corbusier and Pierre Jeanneret, Salon d'Automne, Paris, 1929.

## 16

Appartement = 63 m² 26

SOLARIUM

ture
ale Fernand Léger

GYMNASTIQUE
5,60×4 = 22 m² 40
par
R. HERBST

DOUCHE
TOILETTE

ur de collection
o chstange
à permet de
a enlever

aménagement TSF

REPOS
2 couch. x 130×210 = 38
par
L. SOGNOT

frappé
par F.Léger

SALLE D'ETUDE
4,62 m² × 4 = 19 m² 48
par
Ch Perriand
mur bibliothèque

ensemble réalisé
la collaboration de

R HERBST (groupe U.A.M
Ch. PERRIAND ( " U.A.M

L. SOGNOT ( " U.A.M
LE CORBUSIER groupe U.
P. JEANNERET
F. LEGER (U.A.M et

équipement intérieur (des casiers, des sièges, des tables)
par Le Corbusier P Jeanneret Ch Perriand

[16] Study in the Maison du Jeune Homme ("House for a Young Man"), in collaboration with Le Corbusier and Pierre Jeanneret, 1935. [17] The Perriand-designed kitchen (1952) from the Unité d'Habitation, Marseille, fitted in an apartment of the Unité d'Habitation, Berlin, in 2016. [18] Air France office in London, 1958.

[19, 20] Interior of a Les Arcs apartment, 1969. [21] A room layout with Perriand's designs, Galerie Steph Simon, 1956.

[22] 8 Tabouret Tournant, 1928. [23] 7 Fauteuil Tournant, 1928. [24] Chaise Longue Basculante, 1928.

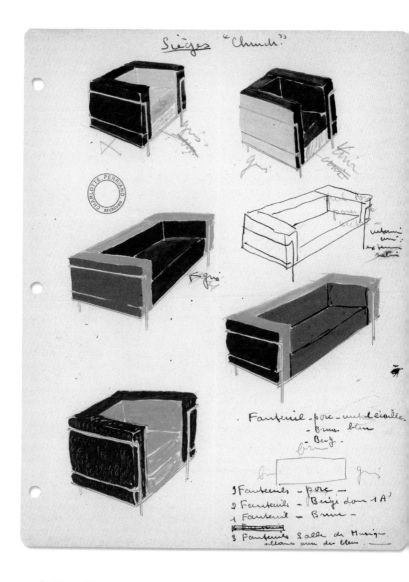

[25] Fauteuil Grand Confort Grand Modèle, 1928. [26] Perriand's drawings of the Grand Confort Grand Modèle. [27] Fauteuil Dossier Basculant, 1929.

[28, 29] Table Extensible 'De Luxe', 1930.

## 32

[30, 31] Credenza, 1931, and shown with bookshelves.  [32] Tokyo Chaise Longue, 1940.

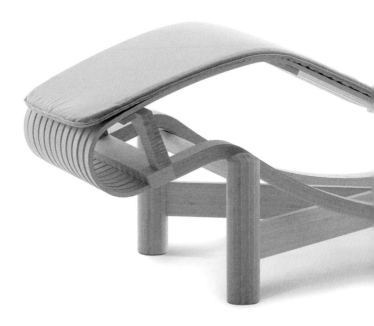

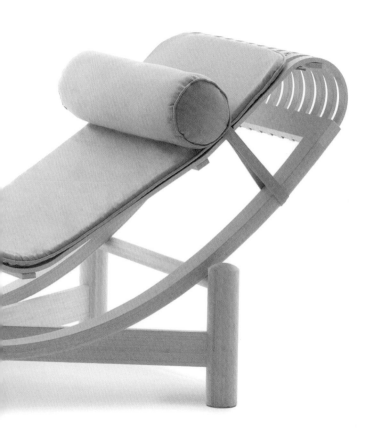

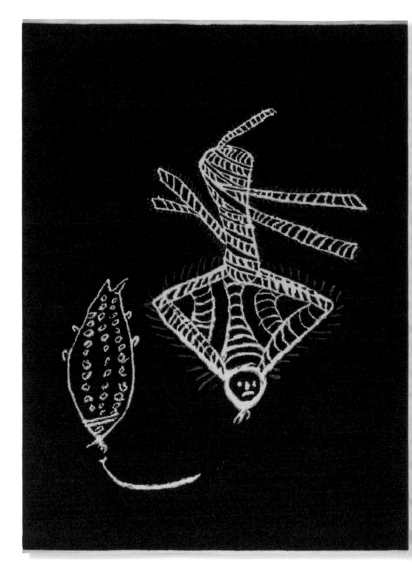

[33] Graffiti rug, 1940. [34] Air France table, 1953.

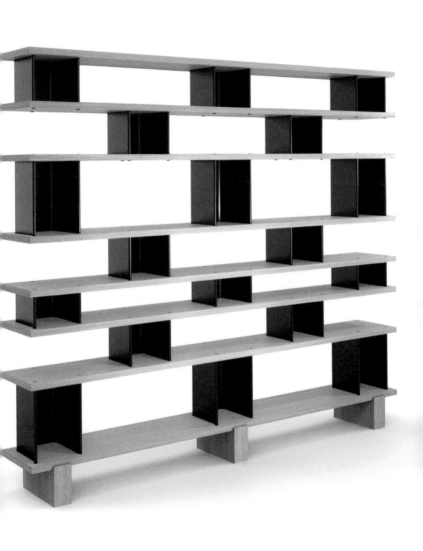

## 38

[35] Graffiti rug with Doron Hotel chair. [36] Doron Hotel armchair, 1947. [37] Nuage à Plots bookcase, 1956. [38] Ombra Tokyo chair, 1954.

[39] Model sitting on a Fauteuil Bas Empilable at the "Proposal for a Synthesis of the Arts" exhibition, Tokyo, 1955. [40] Nemo lighting, 1962.

[41] Rio coffee table, 1962. [42] Ventaglio tables, 1972.

[43, 45] "Charlotte Perriand: The Modern Life", Design Museum, London, 2021.
[44] Perriand's designs displayed in the Museum of Modern Art, New York, 2022.

…nd et le Japon
…saire Takashimaya, Tokyo, 1955
…ynthèse des Arts

[46] "Biennale Des Antiquaires", Grand Palais, Paris, 2008. [47, 48] "Perriand: Inventing a New World", Fondation Louis Vuitton, Paris, 2019–20.

# Picture Credits

The publishers would like to thank the following sources for their kind permission to reproduce the pictures in this book.

[49] Perriand in Japan, 1960.

**MIX**
Paper | Supporting responsible forestry
FSC® C144853
www.fsc.org

Published in 2024 by OH! Life

An imprint of Welbeck Non-Fiction Limited, part of Welbeck Publishing Group. Offices in London, 20 Mortimer Street, London W1T 3JW, and Sydney, Level 17, 207 Kent Street, Sydney NSW 2000 Australia.www.welbeckpublishing.com

Text and Design © Welbeck Non-Fiction Limited 2024

Cover: 7 Fauteuil Tournant by Charlotte Perriand integrated into the Le Corbusier®, Pierre Jeanneret®, Charlotte Perriand® Collection, courtesy of Cassina iMaestri

A CIP catalogue record for this book is available from the British Library.

ISBN 978-1-83861-205-4

Publisher: Lisa Dyer
Contributing writer: Dominic Lutyens
Copyeditor: Katie Hewett
Design: www.gradedesign.com and James Pople
Production controller: Arlene Lestrade

Printed and bound in China

10 9 8 7 6 5 4 3 2 1